The Hero
of the
Revolution
Serves
Us Tea

For Sue —
With gratitude
for your support
and friendship —
Alele
1-21-'14

AUTHOR'S NOTE

Thank you to Jane Hirsfield and B. H. Fairchild for their guidance and encouragement in this project. Thank you to fellow poets and readers Sarah Gordon, Betty Littleton, Lisa Reeves, Lee Ann Pingle, Mary Anne O'Neal, Emily Hipchen, and to my husband Lee, who offered valuable feedback on the poems in the developing manuscript. Many thanks to Peace Corps colleague Connie Goddard, who helped me experience Romania more fully and to the volunteers of Group 27 for support and kindness. Sincere gratitude to editor Sue Walker and her publishing team for patient and thoughtful collaboration. And heartfelt thanks to Veronica Clonda, Mihai and Raluca Jurca, Ana and Petre Puscas, Felicia Vintila, Alina Deliman, Andrada Mezea, Cristina Muresan, and Dr. Traian Orban (the hero, himself), whose lives inspired my writing.

The Hero
of the
Revolution
Serves
Us Tea

Clela Reed

Clela Reed (signature)

Negative Capability
PRESS
MOBILE, ALABAMA

photo by Connie Goddard

A Negative Capability Press Book

Published in the United States of America by
Negative Capability Press
62 Ridgelawn Dr. East
Mobile, AL 36608

Production and design by HTDesignS
Cover & back cover image by Clela Reed
Editing Assistants: Rachael Alex and Corey Harvard

Printed in the United States of America

Scan to visit
www.negativecapabilitypress.org

Scan to visit and like
Negative Capability on Facebook

CONTENTS

*For the people of Romania
who have more courage than they claim,
more strength than they feel,
and greater riches than they recognize.*

PREFACE

Writing here at my window which overlooks the autumn forest of Georgia hardwoods, I must pore over photos, reread blog entries, hear music I played so often during that year to bring back the intensity of my experience in Romania. But now I can add to that the greater appreciation and perspective two years have brought. I understand more fully that the people I met there, the challenges of daily life, the absorption of a different culture were all transformative—inspiring and, in important ways, healing.

My emotional state when I decided to join the Peace Corps was bruised. Yes, serving in the Peace Corps was a childhood dream; yes, I found myself finally at a point in my life where responsibilities wouldn't hold me back, but there was more. In the previous year, within ten months, I had gone through the deaths of five persons close to me: both parents, my brother's wife, my sister-in-law's husband, and a friend of more than thirty years. My parents' deaths, six months apart, came at the end of five years of a heart-sickening downward spiral in which I was earnestly and helplessly involved. My brother Bill was tending his dying wife, and I was left handling all the medical and legal affairs of my parents. A few months before my mother died, my husband's sister learned of the tumor invading her husband's brain. We were in shock that this vigorous man in his prime was gone after four months of useless, but painful, treatments. Shortly after my father's death in the fall, Bill's wife died of lymphoma. And soon after Christmas, our close friend of more than thirty years had a stroke followed by a heart attack and was gone suddenly from our lives. The waves of grief seemed to knock me down each time I tried to stand. In addition to this grief and depression, marital problems plagued us and sent us into counseling to salvage what we had worked to maintain for thirty-six years. In the end, I knew I needed to take some positive action. I knew I wanted to act totally as a single entity, to face challenges, to feel I was doing something worthwhile, to reconnect to who I was when I dreamed of such things before obligations and expectations shaped my course. A quote I've long loved from the Lakota expresses it well: "Sometimes we have to travel to the edge of ourselves to find our center."

The journey was different in many ways than I expected. I had requested a tropical site. But instead of living in a hut in some warm climate, I spent much of the year sloughing to and from my village apartment through snow or rain on broken sidewalks or down city streets lined with either the elaborate art nouveau architecture of Secessionist buildings or the stark and depressing Communist-era bloc apartment buildings. Instead of smiling open faces, I encountered those of the often solemn and purposeful Eastern Europeans. Instead of working with teachers in my official designation as "teacher trainer," I found myself teaching the English words for weather and colors and time to middle school students. The Peace Corps mantra of "Be flexible" rang in my ears. But the experience was—in an overused word—wonderful, certainly full of wonder. I've tried to capture some of that wonder in my poems and blog entry excerpts in this book. The title poem seems an appropriate choice because the humility, courage, and pragmatic attitude of the gentleman who inspired it were evident in so many I met there.

My decision to leave Romania after thirteen months of service was based on my conviction that, as the US government's assessment of the country's need at that time showed and as the situation in my own village confirmed, my presence as a volunteer there was simply not needed. It seemed an indulgence to stay, an unwarranted sacrifice asked of my husband and family. But I've come to realize during these two years since coming home and after two return visits to my site, that even though Romania may not have needed me, I needed Romania.

Sintandrei

Between the city and the village,
a corridor of linden trees divides the fields,
sunflowers from the corn,
makes a passageway of welcome
like the arms of village children held high
for kindergarteners to pass beneath
at the start of each school year.

My first time through, I felt as new
as they, joining something only
conjured. I would see it later
in their faces as they scanned
the schoolyard crowd, wide eyes
fluttering and mouths agape.

I felt it as the driver dodged the potholes
and neared the town through dappled light,
and as the whitewashed trunks of trees
gave way to stuccoed stores on crumbling walks
where benches held the kerchiefed old,

and I felt it as their curious eyes met mine,
this *voluntara Americana*, that a wakening
through confluence — this time, this place,
a unique grace —
awaited.

PROLOGUE

Monday, May 3rd, 2010

Two weeks from tomorrow I'll begin an experience I feel I've been waiting for all my life—even when for long periods of time I didn't think about it or imagine it was possible. As a child during the Kennedy era, I was intrigued with the idea of the newly formed Peace Corps and thought there could be no better way to help others while representing my own country and getting to know the culture of another. In fact, my "senior speech" as I left high school was on the importance of the Peace Corps. Then education, children, career, and failing parents all made two years away seem impossible. In February '09 I came to the sudden realization that I had reached a point in my life where I was free of the responsibilities that made my absence impossible. I retired from teaching, my two sons were grown and on their own, I had no grandchildren, and both my parents, who had needed my help through a difficult final chapter, had died in '08. And, importantly, my husband agreed I should pursue this challenging service.

Lagniappe

It's the way you place the best peach
on the kitchen sill in morning sun,
knowing flesh and juice
beneath its velvet
will distill
soil, water,
blossom and light
into sweetness.

So when you eat it,
striking gold and rose
below inviting skin,
dripping nectar
down your arms,
licking clean the stone,
you consume in swollen
hemispheres
one tender blend,
one peach's universe.

In just this way I've placed
my love for you
in the window of my being,
sunniest spot,
distilling all that shines
in the calling world I roam
into a ripened sweetness,
globe of flavor
you will one day taste,
you may one day
even savor.

Monday, May 3rd, 2010

The application process was thorough, lengthy, and at times frustrating. Essays, letters of recommendation, interviews, fingerprinting, dental and medical screening, and forms, forms, forms. A year ago I became an official "invitee" and was told my medical and dental screening had been approved. My destination was to be Central Asia. For months I waded through Rosetta Stone Russian lessons, thinking that would be the language I'd need. Then in February of this year, I learned my post had been changed to Eastern Europe.

He Says My Fingerprints Are Wearing Off

The chubby cop scurries,
adjusts the machine,
hands me lotion and tissues while
touting his French / German genes
as we reference my government travel,
and then he casually notes
my too-smooth digits
now exposed by the system,
hatless and pink
like ten balding midgets.

      "It happens. The prints wear off.
      Depends on what you do, you know.
      Handle caustics?"
      (Do exfoliates count? lemon juice?
      diaper cream? loofahs? pie dough?)
      "Not really."
      "Well, as you get older,
      they just start to go."

I stand here on what seem two solid feet
whose toes are no doubt losing their prints
and feel myself fading — not even a grin
left behind — as unique loops and lines
of me-ness disappear from my hands,
which hang there, ungroovy and bland.
I take the two cards of ten ovals,
say thanks for gray smudges,
and think Identity Theft indeed
as I turn to leave,
the clock above the door
brazen, ticking loudly
as I go.

TRAINING

Monday, May 31st, 2010

The language instructors are very good, which is fortunate since they have 10 weeks to get us ready to function in our rural villages where very little English will be spoken. The lessons are fast-paced from 8:30 to 12:30 and interactive, so there's no chance of zoning out. At about 11:30 I start feeling my synapses closing down one-by-one like lights going out in a suburban neighborhood.

Friday, September 24th, 2010

In trying to learn the language, I'm surprised at how the words and formations I think I know slip from my brain like eggs from a teflon frying pan. It takes many mnemonic devices to make anything stick.

Limba Romana
(The Romanian Language)

She's not my mother tongue,
nor stepmother even.
She likely wouldn't have me,

> hunkered here on her ancient doorstep,
> mewling vowels that all emerge as "uh,"
> peeling r's from the roof of my mouth
> where I tried to roll them,
> tripping over *pui* and *lui*
> and sputtering sounds of esch and eetz
> where the letters' tails demand.

So I'm just another stray now,
wearing my dejection
like a mangy hide,
but growling at the gravel
all the same,
raising eyes at times
to catch a glimpse
of HER — radiant in her arc
of window,
robed in rich embroidery,
brushing out luxuriance
                  and
> singing,
> always singing
> that haunting,
> beautiful song

with the lyrics I cannot fathom.

Monday, May 31st, 2010

Sometimes in the day-to-day (hour-to-hour!) challenges, something beautiful happens: an old man in a supermarket parking lot feeds stray dogs bread and meat scraps several days last week bits of delicate white fluff from the cottonwood trees swirled all around the campus, drifting into classrooms, sticking in our hair, making lunchtime outside seem like a picnic in a snow globe. And lovely gestures—Felicia's father kissing my hand, and yesterday Martha's gazda gentleman sitting us down at his garden table, spreading out a big map of Romania and giving us a "geography lesson" while his wife served us raspberry ice cream.

Manna
~*Peace Corps Training, Romania, 2010*

The white fluffs — falling, swirling
in the breeze — felt at first like gifts
for our hunger, but we, pouring
from the steam of noonday classrooms,
soon thought of snow, of fresh-fall joy.

We were kids again, escaping
the tedious training, forgetting
for a while the pecking question
of service assignments ahead.
Laughing at the bits stuck in our hair,
on our bread and cheese,
we braved the sowing blizzard!

Those few of us from prairies
knew about cottonwood seeding,
tufts from the catkins released
to the wind and a risky fate,
prized by pioneers for their promise
of firewood and shade.
But, more Romanian to me than American,
snowstorms of tree fluff enchanted me.

We ate our lunch in respite that day,
figurines in a world turned to snow globe.
Or perhaps, after all,
like those wanderers in wilderness,
tasting the manna and trusting fate.

Monday, May 31st, 2010

My morning walk is a pleasant mile or so down a tree-lined boulevard (oaks, maples, cottonwoods, horse chestnuts) until it deadends into a busy street where I cross and walk a short distance. Then I turn right into a busy short cut (haven't decided if it's a street or ally) past storage units and behind bloc apartment buildings and emerge on the street our school is on. From there it's only a block to the entrance of the campus where a security guard bids me Buna dimineata (good morning), recognizing at once that I'm one of "that group." Everyone in the city knows about our program and our three-month presence here. The newspaper published an article about our arrival and apparently to be one of the gazdas is considered an honor. Shop keepers and people on the street are very helpful, and I haven't felt unsafe one moment when I was "slightly" lost after meeting with some of the PCVs for a beer after school one day, I had no trouble communicating with a shop keeper to get directions. We get our share of bemused looks, of course. This is only the second year PC has located the training here and Americans, I take it, aren't usually part of the landscape.

On the Walk from the Training Site
~Peace Corps Training, Romania, 2010

Paint it from memory:
Dab in marigolds, zinnias,
and poppies that flourished
in the black soil by our path.
No matter the background —
cement block edgings, dirty stucco,
and thin, stray dogs sleeping in litter —
the eye finds the bright colors
stippled on gray.

From the flowering dooryards
of bloc apartment buildings
(brush in the watching grannies in black),
the summer-bored children
ran toward us at first sighting,
little paparazzi without cameras,
calling "Hello, hello!" their one
English word.

On crumbling sidewalks
they bounced all about us.
Paint them smiling and blooming,
faces turned upward,
arms reaching to entwine us
and hands waving in sunlight
with the hunger of leaves.

The Weighing
~upon completing Peace Corps training

I never saw her carry her own weight.
She was always seated, delivered there
early in the morning by someone who knew
how small and alone she would look
huddled on the city street, legs and feet
wrapped for warmth, kerchief knotted
beneath her chin — someone's *bunica*
with a bathroom scale and a basket by her side.

Hurrying to my bulging days of language
and enlightenment, gray-concrete protocol
and fine finesse of cultural sensitivity, and
the challenge of endurance for this body
(just reaching womanhood when Kennedy
made the call to look beyond the getting
to the giving) and for this brain which
has never reasoned better, but which
falters now in the quick recall of words
and facts fresh-tucked into the folds,

often I saw my morning walk
as a march of will. It became a rhythmic
chiding that dared me not to whine,
to ignore the pain in my ankle,
or worse, within, to forget the hosts
who didn't want their guest,
to dismiss the coaxing smiles
and my school-girl degradation
when the alien words I wanted to say
weren't there. I could stroll right past
another's pain and scarcely feel the tug.

When it was all over then — final days,
packing up, I passed the *bunica*
one last time and something in me
tipped. I stopped and circled back.
I placed five lei in the tattered basket,
removed my shoes, and stepped onto
the scale. I stood up straight, breathed
in deep and finally weighed it all — three
months of voluntary struggle, doubting
self and Fate and others — weighed it all
and felt its mass, and let it drop away.

"God bless you," I smiled
and touched her shoulder,
as we saw and weighed each other.

SERVICE

Sunday, July 25th, 2010

I'm back at my training site and should be doing my homework, but just had to post a quick entry to say my visit to my assignment site, a village near Oradea, was very informative and thoroughly enjoyable. I was introduced to the mayor, the principal and staff of the school, the other Romanian English teacher, the librarian, police chief, the post mistress, the clerk at the general store, the Orthodox priest, the librarians in Oradea, and a few of the children of the school. The school is a friendly, cheery, clean place with conveniences and modern equipment. V was a great hostess, translator, travel companion (18 hr. train trip north) and tour guide. She and her brother and sister made me feel very welcome. Her dear brother transported me all over the area and lugged my luggage around, which was much appreciated since I was trying to move some of my belongings here for storage until I move down in two weeks. (My lodging is not ready yet, so I and my extra luggage ended up in V's apartment.) V's sister is a gourmet cook and insisted on bringing wonderful dishes over—the last a big tray of her special tiramisu! The librarian and husband had me over for a cookout, and the principal and his wife prepared a multi-course lunch with lemon vodka aperitif and "Bull's Blood" red wine for the meal of traditional meats with cabbage and soup, finishing with fresh fruit. We were instructed that its wise to accept all invitations, but I would have, anyway! Romanians take pride in their cooking and do it well. Overall, I felt very welcomed and quite honestly didn't want to leave. Oradea is very close to my village—only about four miles through fields of sunflowers and corn. It's a fabulous city. Budapest is just over the border and a short drive or train ride away. This is a fine location for visitors to find me (hint, hint). Now, I must do my homework and study so I'll be able to stumble through conversations with the villagers sounding less like a two-yr-old with a speech impediment. Oh, one bit of humor—Peace Corps is Corpul Pacii in Romanian, but some native speakers want to say it in English. At times, after those long train rides and umpteen meetings, being called a Peace Corpse seems altogether fitting.

Tuesday, August 10th, 2010

I'm here! Arrived yesterday morning at 7:00 a.m. and was greeted at the train door (literally) by my ever-cheerful and industrious principal and my sweet and reliable counterpart. The trip this time only took 15 hours because we made a speedy switch at the intervening station. Five of us PCVs were together to this point and had a mountain of luggage among us. So when we learned that three of us had to be on the next platform over, the smart (and strong) youngsters jumped down onto the tracks and made a hand-to-hand luggage brigade to convey the bags to the next platform without having to tackle the two sets of stairs and underpass. My (senior) job was to "guard" the luggage as it stacked up. It worked, our train was on time, and we zipped away (well as zippy as Romanian trains can muster) to cross through Transylvania and the Carpathian mountains on to our three different sites. I was in a sleeper car, but didn't sleep much and then when I arrived at my village and was left in my new home, I was too excited to sleep, so just got back on a regular schedule, waiting until 11:00 p.m. or so for bed time. My apartment defies description, but of course I'll try. It's a large attic apartment (slanting ceilings and dormers everywhere) with lots of space and some really neat features. It also has no light fixtures—only wires with light bulbs—and no screens on the huge and numerous windows. It's been partially remodeled recently and isn't finished. I keep getting assurances that it will all be done soon. In the meantime, after a night of frequent encounters with the local little vampires, I've pulled out the official Peace Corps mosquito net and have asked for a hook so that I can hang it. A family of four occupies the first two floors—lovely folks who are making me squeeze out every Romanian word and phrase I can remember. But as to the apartment in the big red house on the outskirts of town, the only thing that keeps coming to mind is "teetering on the brink of elegance." . . . After the meeting I ventured to the magazine (small store) on the way home to buy some provisions. Realizing I had not brought my shopping bag with me, I decided to buy a bucket, knowing I would surely need one. So there I was walking back to my red house along the main road, carrying my bucket overflowing with bread, water, fruit, cheese, and some wild flowers I picked along the way. Later, I repeated the process at the other magazine (there are two in town), this time carrying a red, plastic laundry tub filled with cleanser, toilet paper, oranges, bananas, pretzels, and a bottle of wine and walking down different streets, saying Buna Ziua (hello) to all the curious folks I encountered. I introduced myself to the clerks at both stores and explained in Romanian what I was doing in their village. Integration is key. Oh, yeah, they're getting to know me, all right.

The Blessing of the Baggie
(in a country where they can't be bought)

Oh, virgin zip-lock baggie I take from the drawer,
(thirty-third in my limited collection) fresh
and satin smooth, may you serve long and well.

May you hold leftovers with no evident drips,
may you keep grapes and plums firm and whole
while bouncing in my school bag pocket,
may you save my croissant from the blight of stale
and hold my crisp crackers in dryness.
May you handle wipes that are wet and tubes
wont to drip and keep various baubles well bundled.

And may your washings be many and clear,
your integrity solid and true as you
dry on your wooden spoon pedestal,
inside out, chaste in evaporation.
May your zippy lips continue to match,
your seamy parts bonded for good.

And when at last you reach the inevitable
ending — leaking seam or stubborn stench or
zip that's sadly lockless — may you, Oh 33rd from
the drawer of Vesta, be held above the trash bin's
rim, honored with a sigh, then let fall, maiden to the pit,
your loss bemoaned, your service well saluted.

Bananas in Romania

Plump fingers curve and clutch
rims of bins in even the smallest stores
in the most remote villages.
They keep their hold,
take their place with coffee,
eggs, bread, cheese —
the staples with no season.
Romanians just can't get enough
of what so long they couldn't . . .

unless one had a means.
The grocer's grown-up son
relates with reticence how
once in Ceausescu's hungry
times, he took a ripened one
from his father's hidden stash
and sat on the courtyard bench,
swinging legs and innocence,
as natural as any primate
savoring his prize. But soon
from windows all around
angry calls and curses shot down
and sent him crying back inside.

Years later he would comprehend:
"It was not that they begrudged
my luck. They knew we had bananas.
It was that I mocked their deprivation,
eating the fruit before them."

Friday, September 3rd, 2010

Lee left this morning and the apartment seems cold and quiet. We had a fine three-week visit and he's planning to return in December. Our communication, of course, is very good with Skype and email, but they do little to keep my toes warm. How fortunate I am to have a husband who understands and supports my unconventional aspirations.

Retrospective
~for Lee

Vantage point and impact mark them,
the times I clearly watch myself
below as though I sit high on some
camera crane or hover in a basket
swung beneath a bright balloon,
silently observant,
aware of some new knowing
at that time, the only time
my conscious self
takes flight, a voyeur of my life
it seems, like

seeing me at twelve blink
and know that childhood days
were over, watching from above
the cornfield where the games
of quick pretend ended —
the sadness spawning wonder,

and me crazy-falling down a slope,
six breaks before I stop
in a spray of powdery white,
and again in white with you
on the foggy lake at sunrise,
waiting for the minister to come.

Another time I'm full of tears
on the yellow hill,
gray stacked above me,
below, the bodies of my parents,
newly lowered, the sharp-carved
record of their time on earth
etched on more than stone,
and just last month, I see
myself below, alone

on the pebble road beneath
raw-dawning skies, wind against me,
as I return from the stop
where you still stood, waiting
for the bus that would take you
to the city, the train, then the plane
that would whisk you half a world
away from me. I see myself a thing undone,
arms wrapped tight so I won't unravel,
the warmth of you all but gone
before I reach the gate.

Zones

When it's 2:00 p.m. here,
it's 7:00 a.m. there.
I picture the earth in laborious rotation,
which, actually, you've always declared too fast
as your shutter snaps at the horizon
where what we quaintly describe
as the sun setting
is earth's turning away.

It's just risen there,
or the earth has turned just enough
to let the sun's light fall upon your face,
our bed, to let you know
I've already taught six classes
and am trying to fill remaining Romanian hours
with a practiced busy-ness,
with whatever glues together this now to that then

when we'll talk —
impulses blipped through space,
the best we can do
when it's 2:00 p.m. there
and 9:00 p.m. here,
and we pretend it doesn't matter
as long as we can speak of what does,
the earth having no intention of stopping
for either of us.

Monday, September 13th, 2010

One of the volunteers in Group 26 and his director (principal) took it upon themselves to invite all the volunteers serving in northwest Romania (10 of us scattered about) to a weekend of getting acquainted—26ers, 27s and a few 25s—before we get too busy with our teaching assignments. . . . While it was fun seeing 27s again (my group who spent the summer in training) and getting to know the others, the "field trips" we took were splendidly interesting and fun. The person largely responsible for this was the director of the school. Not only does he successfully manage a school that shines with careful maintenance, innovative programs, bright and cheerful facilities, and an obviously dedicated staff and faculty, but he also serves as "voluntary executive administrator" of a self-sustaining, totally-organic farm where the workers are graduates of his school's vocational program, plying their skills in all seasons to tend crops, hot houses, animals, and to build furniture, preserve food, and make brooms. We were each given a dandy little whisk broom (because traveling with a long one would be just too Harry-Potterish). When the dear man has spare moments, he retires with his wife and four-yr-old daughter to his cabana (weekend retreat) where he tends various fruit trees and grapes. Here he, his wife and some staff members hosted a gratar (cookout) for us, complete with his own tuica (a kind of plum brandy) and wine from his grapes. We also were free to take walks around the hilly and beautiful property, and I was actually able to hug one of those Romanian haystacks I love.

Haystacks in Romania

To build them
is both chore and celebration.
      Someone stands the needle
and the stack is built around it, hay
from summer's fields of rain and sun,
grasses bred, cut by hand, then dried
and raked on soil dark as blood.

Forkful by forkful they feed the stack
first onto a collar of branches
      laid to let it breathe.
Then up and up —
  the wife or daughter
      rides the swell,
      tromps the grains
          as the pile peaks,
then waits in triumph, perched,
to be laddered down
at the end.

Finally, they comb the shaggy mound,
      stems down to shed rain
      and melting snow,
and crown it with a wreath of sturdy vines.
And there stands Life preserved
      for winter's stock
who in turn will nurture life.
Nothing changes through the ages.
Women bring out savory pies,
      someone's uncle plays a tune,
and young men clink *palinka* with the old.

I would join them if I could
      for love of scattered haystacks.

Moonlit or hooded bright with snow,
the stacks stand still against trees gold
or ever green or mountains blue with smoke.
        I take a hundred pictures.
What is it — this allure of haystacks?

Their silhouettes inhabit fields
like watchmen
            hunkered in wool cloaks
or wizards in enchanted robes.
        But, no, if magic,
                    it must be of the female earth,
the stacks' anatomy of mother bounty
casting spells of that familiar comfort
        sure survival brings,
ancient incantations sounding always
like the lullaby of spring.

Saturday, November 13th, 2010

I've come to a better understanding of the importance of the church as a constant in the lives of people who have endured feudal lords, barbaric invasions, vicious monarchs, dictators, communism, frequent redrawing of country borders to add or subtract large tracts of land and ethnic populations, and rampant government corruption. The church has been a presence from the earliest times and has survived even through the years of atheist communist rule, by means not always noble but certainly pragmatic, in order to keep church doors open and parishioners served. It's a quintessentially paternalistic institution—for the 87% of the Romanian population who identify themselves as Orthodox—a symbol of nationalism, its beautiful churches and cathedrals aesthetic foils to the horrors of communist architecture, its solemn traditions and elaborate ceremonies points of pride. It serves an important role in Romanian life and has offered stability and order where other institutions have failed.

Devotion

In Communist Romania, fearing the *Securitate*,
     the Orthodox faithful made the sign of the cross
          in their mouths, with their tongues.

Passing a cemetery or church, they performed
     in secret this act of reverence, a discipline
          learned before they learned their letters.

Today the streets fill with the banners, flowers
     and incense of brocaded processions, with
          the priests' deep chanting and the tolling

of bells, ceremonies to lace up the everyday lives
     of the people into handsome shoes that might carry
          them forward in open step with their neighbors.

          Yet amid such display swells growing nostalgia
     for the past when cloaked faith dared to demand
those acts of devotion for no one but God.

Monday, December 10th, 2010

So the Christmas season is upon us. Pigs are being slaughtered all over Romania with family members helping butcher and prepare the meat in sausages or hams for smoking or freezing. It's a tradition that occurs sometime after Saint Nicholas Day on December 6 and Christmas. This is also the time when children begin caroling through the village, carrying branches with foil stars attached and singing "star carols." I was feeling a bit left out of the gifting of St. Nick's Day when children (and grown up children) receive small gifts in their shoes. But my landlady dashed down the stairs and presented me with a lovely wool felt hat as I was waiting in the foyer for the taxi to the city and then the bus to the PC meeting in Sibiu. And Sibiu with its lovely decorated square and with the snow that has fallen in the past week, I'm starting to put some jolly in my jingle. Oradea has a coating, too, and today for the first time I had to walk my 4K in snow and slush and with flurries flurrying. I was relieved to find that my pricey Geox boots do indeed stay 100% dry inside and have fine traction. (Thanks to Joe R for the recommendation via his wife Diane.) I came home and strung up some lights in a window, put on some holiday music, and started a big pot of soup . . . I have to say though that what really hit me full-force in terms of "the spirit" and what surprised me in my reaction was today's rehearsal for the community program this Friday. I lost it, quite frankly, when I heard the sweet voices of those Romanian children singing "White Christmas." I had to excuse myself to my office momentarily where the documentarian followed me, gave me a big hug, and told me to be strong. It was such a Romanian gesture. I laughed and wiped my eyes and returned for a rousing

"Jingle Bells" where I made the children do the sub-text "Ha, ha, ha" after "laughing all the way." I had bought a pretty red wooden, jingle bell "rattle" in Sibiu with the idea that it would be perfect for the percussion and it was/is! The program at the community center will consist of a dance number (we have quite a talented troupe and a creative media specialist who choreographs) where worldly souls are visited by angels who set them straight, carols and songs in both English and Romanian, and Christmas poems in both languages. Apparently we'll have a visit by Santa Claus (the mayor, I think). And my husband will arrive on Thursday and be here for the program. His visit is anticipated by the village, too. Perhaps I should insist he wear a Santa hat and laugh alot. Joy to the world--all over—in whatever land you're reading this. This season of love and peace has meaning for us all.

Friday, December 31st, 2010

. . . And then our son Dan arrived from California. Lee and I had bought a small tree and decorated it and had lights in the landing window outside our flat, a star wreath on the door. I was disappointed the snow had melted, but he got to experience plenty starting the day after Christmas. On Christmas Eve we had the great pleasure of accepting an invitation through my friend/ colleague Connie to spend the afternoon and evening in a village just south of Oradea. Our hosts (friends of Connie's) were warm-hearted Romanians who had spent some time in the US and spoke very good English. They wanted us to experience the carolers, food, and traditions of their village. Lucky us! The food was a feast of all things Romanian, the homemade wine and polinka well-done, and the walk through the little town with a visit to the Orthodox Church and its priest was a highlight. The priest is an accomplished architect and artist and is adorning the interior of the domed sanctuary in colorful, accurately portrayed iconic paintings. Hes been working on this project in faith and artistry for a few years now and is determined to complete the task. Hes created a space for worship filled with joy—colorful, light, and welcoming. He also had us join him in the parsonage for a sip of polinka and/or homemade wine from his grapes. While there, carolers visited—one of three carolings of the evening. Different from the Dickensian singers with choir-like decorum (our British/American ideals), the carolers here are revelers, often wearing animal or demon masks, wearing fur capes, beating drums, and acting out cautionary tales. Someone always seems to represent good, too—a priest-like character in white who carries a replica of the church constructed of cardboard and foil. Often foil stars attached to a branch are carried, too. We were told the masks and capes were passed down from one generation to the next in a family, along with the particular role. (In a restaurant in Oradea on the 23rd, we were visited by strolling carolers who sang, acted, and danced the "goat dance," something I want to learn more about.) Another group we encountered on our walk—teens led by a different priest—seemed less costumed and medieval, but were just as eager in their singing. It has become more and more clear to me that singing is a very Romanian way to give of oneself. A gift of song is always the right size, always appropriate, always from the heart.

December

It's always been about some star —
this welling joy in slant-light days
and countering of longest nights
with something 'kin to peace.

Before — the old relief, the cycle's tip,
our star's return to coax the seeds and warm
the sap, to stir the sleeping ram to sow
his crop of springtime lambs.

And later — looking East in darkest night,
we found the radiant point, the journey's start
to truth (once known, too evergreen to die)
and love too bright to dim.

It's always been about some star —
some cosmic, mythic, sacred star we hold
when days like these are pale-beam cold and slight,
for in that star is hope.

Sunday, January 16th, 2010

Several of you have asked about my poetry writing. I was quite prolific back in the states and would feel very antsy if two weeks went by and I hadn't written a new poem. It's different here— even if I have some time to write (as I clearly do at the moment), the climate of my brain is not always "right" for poetry. However, I have written a few that I'll hang on to for the possibility of future publication. . . . As I struggle with learning Romanian, I was especially touched when a friend said not to worry, that poetry was my true language. I was reminded of this when reading Romanian poet Nina Cassian's beautifully translated poetry (a gift from Lee). She rhapsodizes about her devotion to her language as she speaks of the " . . . clitoris in my throat/vibrating, sensitive, pulsating,/exploding in the orgasm of Romanian." Oh, dear Nina, I'm afraid I've scarcely begun the foreplay!

Five-Thirty

A mind too long without poetry
loses liquid running,
takes a form more rigid
and becomes the paddock wall
that keeps things out,
that keeps things in.
And then the wind is only wind,
the flickering gloss of leaves
just a cause to frown, and the clouds
that block the sun and the ice
that chokes the pond
have nothing to do
with the climate of the heart,
which is only a pump, after all,
pulling in and pulsing out
whatever it is given.

At times I've seen in memory
the broad shadow cast by camphor trees
advance across the playing field
of my childhood and have remembered
only the welcomed breeze,
our game of flies and grounders
with its sweaty triumphs, long
gulps from a sun-warmed hose,
the way our calloused feet
pounded the earth
when we ran home to supper.

Tuesday, February 1st, 2011

I live in a crystalline world—frigid and brittle. Snow and ice in frozen layers on stem, twig and fence post. I have the feeling that if I poke my head out the window and scream, everything would shatter and fall tinkling into a mound of glitter.

Stasis

Above the plains of snow,
time hovers like a great shield
between this moment
and all that follows.
For once, no Hungarian wind,
no barking dogs,
no clop of hooves before the loaded *caruta*.
Time stretches and thins in the cold white air.

Earth forms crystal at its core
and stops,
and I become so small
within the stillness
that if I open my mouth to speak,
I would only make a breezy exhalation,
a whistling breath

that could be heard by your ears alone
a continent and an ocean away
when the shield lifts
and the indifferent,
noisy spin continues.
It would be precisely then
that you, intent on a close shave
or a well-built Reuben,
would pause, tilt your head toward
 a slight breeze on your ear,
and hear whispered intimacies
impossibly familiar.

Thursday, February 10th, 2010

Walking into the office of my friend, the media specialist, this afternoon, I threw up my hands and laughed, "I used to love Valentine's Day!" I'm valentined to bits, up-to-here with paper, scissors, glue, and glitter, over-glazed with cookie hearts and sprinkles. In short, I've had a "heart attack." And it's only February 10th! But I wanted all my students to know the legend of St. Valentine (16 class periods of that) and make valentines and have a cookie, so I had to do it this week. It's funny how we take our customs for granted until we try to help others understand and appreciate them. Actually, the Romanians have their own celebration of love in February, on the 24th. It's called Dragobete after their version of Cupid, god of love. It's an ancient holiday that apparently was all but ignored during the communist era, but is making quite a comeback as a reaction to the increasing interest in Valentine's Day. Dragobete is related to nature more than our holiday. Supposedly, February 24th is when the birds choose their mates for the spring nest-building and reproducing. In ancient times the young people of the village would go into the forests and fields to find the first snow-drops or violets or any sign of spring. There they were encouraged to make promises of betrothals on that day to insure the protection of the gods. If snow was on the ground, the maidens collected it and melted it. The water was believed to have magical powers and was used in love potions and to wash their hair to make them especially appealing to the young men. If a woman wanted to be loving and alluring all year, she was supposed to touch a man from another village on that day (Where? one wonders) To determine who would be the dominant partner, a couple took part in a "foot-upon-foot" maneuver. Today the holiday seems very much like our Valentine's Day though less commercial, and the cards I've located online are all nature-centered with the earliest tiny flowers and matrimonial birdies—all very sweet and delicate. So my introduction of our silly little valentines ("Bee Mine" with a buzzing bee and tulips, "You're a dear" with a doe holding a valentine, "Whale You Be Mine?" with a whale spouting valentines) took a bit of explaining. "Gluma (joke)," I would say, "It's a joke, see?" A few would get it, but cross-culture puns are hard. The highlight of my three-day marathon was when I told one class as they were finishing up that now they had pretty felicitare (cards) to give to someone they loved. One by one they each brought me one of their cards, complete with hugs and double-kisses. Well, maybe I do still like this holiday after all.

Scattered

Ignore the eight pointing thorns
      of the compass rose.
The day my necklace broke,
the stone beads sprayed
        in fifty different directions,
sending my students scurrying on hands and knees
in happy retrieval, more fun than grammar rules.

I remember when scattering was like that —
for seeds, rose petals, confetti, bread crumbs for the birds,
and sometimes broken strands of beads.

More and more
      so many I love are apart from me —
in other towns, other states, other lands,
and some, other realms
      without a compass rose.

I miss the squeeze of the hand, the hug,
the tactile talk beyond the breath,
      the simple dialogue of skin.
I would have them brought to me
the way the children brought the beads that day,
gathered from all directions,
my body's warmth still in them.

February 27th, 2011

With unaccustomed accuracy, the meteorologist got it right last weekend. Timisoara was as rainy and cold as predicted. As antidote to the weather, however, my PCV colleague Connie and I experienced many sunny moments of extreme generosity and kindness during our visit. . . . The amazing variety in the architecture of the Secessionist buildings—all unique, colorful, often whimsical— and the sheer size of many of the mansions and cathedrals kept us in awe. The city is grandly laid out with stately squares and small residential parks. It was the first city in Europe to light its streets with electricity, and the large elaborate street lamps in the main square (though only old in appearance) attest to the pride in this fact. Another point of pride is that Timisoara is where the 1989 revolution against Ceausescu and the communist regime began. What seemed a spontaneous protest by thousands of the citizens had been building and organizing for some time. Their courage was immense as they faced the tanks and guns, and many lost their lives or were badly injured. One such man who walks with a cane due to having taken two bullets in his leg is the curator/proprietor of the Revolutionary Museum. He, too, showed us uncommon kindness as he patiently took us through two levels of rooms surrounding a courtyard, which also housed exhibits, and explained the significance of the pieces. Sculptures, carvings and paintings that depicted the events of the revolution showed both artistry and reverence for the sacrifices and bravery of the people. The curator had a soft-spoken dignity and humility, and it seemed to me HE was the greatest feature of the museum. He seated us in a small theater to watch a video about the revolution and then disappeared to return with a tray holding two cups of herbal tea. I've certainly never been served tea in a museum before and we found it especially nice on a cold, wet day. It was his birthday, he admitted at the end of our tour, and we were invited into his living quarters briefly where we were given more information in pamphlets as we said our goodbyes. I will no doubt forget the murals, the bell of freedom, and other tributes in the museum, but I'll never forget this man. Connie captured his back in a photo. He didn't want to be photographed because he said the museum wasn't about him. Oh, but it was, dear fellow, it was.

The Hero of the Revolution Serves Us Tea

at Muzeul Revolutiei in Timisoara,
and we are glad for the warmth
as winter rain on the windows blurs
the streets below. We give crumbs of thanks
in our weak Romanian as he retrieves his cane,
removes the tray, and leaves to start the film.

> *This we had not expected, my friend*
> *and I—when we splashed down unfamiliar*
> *sidewalks, map in hand—this private tour,*
> *this old man's greeting at the locked-tight door*
> *that shielded the museum, more a home than*
> *public space within this busy city, his leaning*
> *out the window above to see just who we were.*
>
> *We were shown the artifacts of war,*
> *the uniforms and weapons, panoramic photos*
> *of streets clotted with tanks, choked with mobs*
> *on that Christmas Eve of '89 when patience died.*
> *What moved us more were the carvings,*
> *paintings, ceramics, reminders of how beauty*
> *blooms from pain, and the startling drawings*
> *by children that honored best the risk with their*
> *vivid chalk-and-tempera bodies dwarfed*
> *by black-ink metal monsters.*
>
> *Eventually we find it's true—he was there*
> *that day and marched beneath the flag-with-the-hole*
> *and faced the pivoting eyes of the tanks. His leg, hit*
> *and poorly mended, bears his dignity with a limp.*

We finish the film. Gathering up
umbrellas and coats, we see he's returned.
"Come, I'll give you cards downstairs."
We follow to his private quarters where

the beaming housekeeper makes his lunch,
special, for it's his birthday, she explains.
He is older than the years he tells us.
We want to take his picture, but he waves
our cameras aside.
"This museum is not about me."
And for the first time all afternoon,
we doubt the truth of what he says.

Tuesday, February 1st, 2011

These are the days of layers: underwear, silk long johns, turtleneck sweater, pants, cardigan, coat, scarf, hood over hat, mittens over gloves, boots over multiple socks. And in my mind, too, concerns build up in layers: family, friends, students, colleagues, PC forms, PC projects, PC goals, health, travel. Somewhere under it all I breathe and the essential me (love, laughter, music, poetry) taps out a cardiac rhythm on that old bongo drum, and I abide.

Winter Layering

Layers of ice flocked with layers of snow,
encasing twigs and stems
like stockings and opera gloves
on limbs of the fashionably thin,
take on a disguise of softness.
The world outside my window
wears white velvet over glass.

And I must build my layers, too,
of silk and wool, leather and down
to carry me through the cold outside
from the certain warmth of here
to the thawing warmth of there
when the sun is low and quick.
I hurry ahead of night.

Other layers no one sees,
my inner banks of winter clouds,
my gray on gray tomorrows,
my heavy atmosphere of past,
my sorrows. These I wear within,
but beneath abides the me
who breathes, regardless, in the dark,
who keeps a marching beat
on that ruddy old bongo, tapping away
the cold and gray, drumming in the light.

The Pecan

I reach into my purse or pocket
at the bus stop or in the market
of this place so far from home
and touch the pecan I carry,
finger its smooth shell or bury it
for a moment in my palm.

Pecans from my father's orchard, full and rich,
he and I picked, shelled, and bagged as gifts
for neighbors while he was still able
in those final days as casseroles appeared
silently as manna on his breezeway table.

Before driving away from my
childhood home that day —
October dusk with no moon rising
and a first-frost chill in the breeze —
on some orphan impulse I stooped
and picked up the pecan, a reminder
of our time together, his muted
strength, self-reliant as his trees.

Touching it has become my habit,
a connection to the daughter self
I was before and more —
an emblem of his honor and largesse,
and above all, love,
the necessary seed.

Sunday, March 6th, 2011

The weather has been just awful—dreary gray and cold, fog or mist or snow in the mornings, mud and overcast skies in the afternoons. We've had so little sun here in the past few months. I've become fairly neurotic about my sun hunger. If there is a ray peeking through and I'm home, I'll grab my sunglasses and peel off as much as I can get away with without neighborhood scandal and sit on the end of my desk at the big window there. I pretend I'm a solar cell and imagine the light seeping into my bones where it will store. I wrote a poem about a fire eater this week, I read travel guides on Spain, and I taught my students two sunshine songs. Yes, I know it sounds desperate, but somehow singing about sunshine seemed to create the illusion. So I mugged, mimed, and otherwise entertained as I sang "Let the sunshine in, face it with a grin," and "You are my sunshine, my only sunshine." Interestingly, they had a difficult time saying "sunshine," which is surprising since the "sh" sound is so prevalent in their language. Anyway, they seemed to enjoy it and paid polite though clueless attention when I tried to explain Seasonal Affective Disorder.

Fire Eater

Hollowed out from winter,
drained to gray and grayer,
I'm hungry for the sun.

I will be an eater of flames,
tilt my face toward the sky,
lift a long, long-handled spoon
and scoop the orange and yellow
into bites of light I'll swallow
until I begin to shine!
Then all will know
what I've been dipping into.

I want to give off summer heat,
so even walking in the snow,
buttercups and marigolds
will blossom at my feet.

And I want to feast
so quick in famished greed
that scattered light-crumbs
from my mouth will feed
the pecking, weary birds
and lift them into spring.

Sunday, March 27th, 2011

. . . And the week held some down moments, too, part of the "mixt" package. It's always true that we alone are ultimately responsible for our own happiness. But it seems that when you're thousands of miles from home, speak little of the local language, have a host of expectations placed on you, and are not even sure what you're doing is really needed, that the "alone" part gets pretty heavy, and as one PCV friend put it, it's enough just to keep from going crazy. And that's why God gave us chocolate, Vivaldi, poetry, Kindles, and a little Transylvanian white wine.

Balance

In those scant-light days of Romanian winter,
she imagined happiness a big orange tabby
she could coax into her lap through devices —
a favorite ballad plugged into her ears,
a glass of vin alb in her hand,
a beam of afternoon sun illuminating
one spot in her flat where she could pull a chair.
She knew how to will the purr.

                    The panic of loneliness was the mouse hiding
                              under the bed, in the hall closet,
                         darting across the floor and visible
                                   often in her periphery,
                             gnawing at her courage
                                      in dark places
                              with tiny vicious teeth
                                    she could hear
                                    if she let herself,

            but she didn't.
       The cat grew fat with mice,
    and winter ended on the muddy plain
       just as it always had. She left
    and returned to her old life, awaking
  to find herself in a grocery with gleaming floors,
 wondering where they'd moved the peanut butter,
   noticing a new array of organic choices as she
    loaded her cart with food for more than one,
         knowing she could drive it home,
            her moon-roof filled
                 with sun.

Tuesday, April 12th, 2011

Alas, the few days of sun last week are history. I caught some lovely sunsets, but now we are in a solid week of rain with temps in the mid 30s at night and the low 50s in the day. It's supposed to clear by Saturday, which will be wonderful because it's the christening day (or blessing day) of baby Elijah, the son of the foster parents at the Roma Boys School where I am volunteer tutoring. It will be at the small Baptist Church in our village and I've been invited to attend. Let the sun shine in!

Holy Child

We think of the guiding star and angels
proclaiming the news of His birth —
He who would lift the shadows,
teach charity, give hope,
His arrival changing
the very numbering of Time.

But look into the eyes of any
infant someone. Beyond the spark
of blue or brown, deep into the waiting
innocence of the green-grass soul,
we glimpse what we embody
from our start, tinder for unfathomable light,
fire, and the paradox of burning.

Every child is a holy child,
one more filament of God
to be entered into county records,
announced in narrow columns, page six
of the local paper, where we squint
to read the host of names printed there
in a small and quiet font.

Saturday, April 16th, 2011

It's spring. Quick! Paint the trees! Everywhere—tree trunks are freshly whitewashed. I (and apparently many others, according to a web search) question the practice. Answers and theories vary widely—many I had already heard from Romanians I asked. Top of the list is that the wash is an insecticide, that it prevents crawling critters from reaching the leaves and fruit to do their damage. Next in popularity is that it protects the bark from "scalding" from the sun, followed by weather-fluctuation protection (bark being damaged by the quick change from freezing temps at night to the daytime warmth of spring sun). But I like the unguarded, honest answer someone let slip out—it just looks neat and tidy, like the trees are cleaned up and fresh. And not just the trees either. Notice the concrete communist-era utility poles with their fresh stockings. I really doubt the insects will bother them, right? They just look cleaner. This seems fitting for a country fairly obsessed with cleanliness in their homes and yards and in their personal hygiene. . . . For many Romanians keeping body, clothes and home clean is a major accomplishment and they do it very well. The women take housekeeping seriously and spend inordinate amounts of time making sure the floors and bathrooms—in particular—are clean. No one wears shoes in the home, and slippers are often provided for guests. (If I were an entrepreneur in Romania, I'd start a charming line of guests' slippers in all sizes and styles, washable and snuggly.) Effective cleaning products here are all but canonized, spoken about in reverent whispers—no kidding! So, I salute the clean Romanians and marvel at their resolve. If Cleanliness-is-Next-to-Godliness, then they certainly have a nod from our Maker. Unfortunately, these good habits have not ventured out to where litter abounds at roadsides and fields. But then, the white-stockinged trees preside there, giving perhaps a little inspiration.

Presenting the White-washed Trees of Spring

I want to see those Romanian trees
dance a can-can, sassy as you please,
shake leafy heads and kick in time
their new white stockings in a chorus line,

or see one or two step up to the mic,
(clinging strapless gowns of white
all the way to the mossy floor),
croon 'til the crowds cry out for more.

Or watch them parade in military whites,
single file in the morning light,
then wait at attention by the busy road
for some "At ease!" never crowed.

Those trees, white stockinged,
white gowned, and white suited
could spice up Romania
if they just weren't so rooted.

Dust

It dulls the dark-grained surfaces
of desk and shelves, table tops
and window sills, settles on the humming,
oblivious fridge and the headboard
just above my pillow. I sweep it up,
swipe it down, sneeze into its grainy
cloud and wonder where it comes from,
how it finds its way to the third floor
where windows stay closed all winter,
where only I abide.

There's the answer! I've read that
two million dead cells drift from
our skin each hour. Each hour!
I'm sweeping up a mess of me,
an epidermal dust storm in a day!
Regeneration less than tidy —
inside as well as out. Cells shed,
new ones grow in bone and belly,
lung and liver — sure compliance to
a blueprint slow to fade.

After all these sloughing seasons, then,
when I've boxed mementos,
double kissed farewells, and
left this place that tests my will,
will I come home a different me,
gleaming on your doorstep,
my old self bit-by-bit discarded,
bagged and yellow-tied in the weekly trash?

Monday, June 20th, 2011

There are so many reasons I'd like to stay in this beautiful and complex country, enjoying its people, countryside, food, music, and traditions. I like my Red House apartment, the big-sky sunsets, and many special people in my village and in the city.

Views

". . . once you've gotten used to wide plains and long sightlines, it's annoying to have everything folded in on you. Boxlike shrubbery and cloistering trees. . . . It makes me uneasy." Annie Proulx

Newfoundland left her sky-drunk,
a forest creature struck delirious
in fields of light, clouds, and stretching sea
that changed her very breathing.
So how to abide the vault of green Vermont
or even its white-flocked limbs in winter,
arced above her like a brittle threat?
This, her childhood land, unnerved her.
She moved to wide Wyoming.

But for my mother, brought to that hill
on Alabama plains, the great blue dome
implied a perilous exposure,
nowhere to be found the sheltering mountains
of her childhood, peaks of Wasatch
cradling her in canyon shadows.
Nowhere, too, the towers
of her San Francisco, steel and granite comfort
through adolescence, family deaths,
wartime marriage, and the darkened panes
of air raid drills.

She feared the sky and what it held.
"Run," she told us, "if you see a dark cloud funnel,
run to the nearest ditch. It's all we have."
Our road bed, deep and sandy, good for play,
was edged with banks I came to see as shields.
But for the threat of hurricanes, she braced

our home so well it became a fortress for our kin.
Oh Mother! How she tried to banish sky —
the trellises and arbors, the oaks, pears, and pines,
the shutters and dark drapery! I understand now

why I've tried to get it back. Why living
in my forest home for many years and counting
requires discrete sabbaticals of sky, rendezvous
with moon and stars at beach or mountain top,
and lately one full year of riotous sunsets,
gypsy clouds above the Hungarian plains
that filled my tallest window's view.

If only we had stood there,
Annie, Mother, and I, watching
the highest layer of clouds light up
with gold and rose, birds weaving rays
into song and flight.
"Just look!" we'd have said,
our arms around my mother
as we showed her how everything
is more radiant and worthy
in such extravagance of sky.
Standing there — bold, unfolded,
open-eyed with night descending —
we'd have made her feel safe.
We'd have taught her to breathe.

Saturday, July 17th, 2010

I've met my counterpart and she's terrific! Flavia is intelligent, understanding, attractive and just idealistic enough to make a great partner for forward-thinking projects. We both love Hemingway, poetry, movies and Sandra Bullock. Neither of us has ever been able to keep pet fish alive and after getting lost on our way back from the train station to the university (when we decided to use our two-hour lunch to purchase our tickets for Monday night's fifteen-hour train trip) we confessed that neither of us has a smidgen of directional sense. I really like this young woman and want my son Dan to visit soon. (I know, I know—but mother knows best.)

Monday, May 2nd, 2011

. . . For it was MAY DAY in Romania and at their garden cottage in the hills above Oradea, Raluca and her husband hosted a fine celebration of all things associated with this day—a salute to laborers (Labor Day in much of Europe), spring and all its fertile promise, and the honoring of the dead (the Orthodox version of the Catholic observance in November). Mostly it was a grand excuse for a party! I've decided that Raluca—brilliant teacher of French and English, reader, traveler, gourmet cook, skilled organizer—is a sort of Romanian Gertrude Stein who seems to gather up interesting friends and acquaintances in the great vortex of her energetic hospitality. She and her husband had just returned from ten days in Spain but managed to have everything ready and perfect for the gathering on Sunday. Today she had to be back in the classroom! . . . And speaking of the courses, first: coffee and tuica (brandy) with herb biscuits, then: a spread of many appetizers from homemade bread with zacusa (sweet pepper and eggplant condiment) to all sorts of pickled and fresh vegetables and aged sausages, next: a wonderful soup—a Romanian version of the Hungarian goulash—with chicken, peppers, carrots, onions, and all-important paprika and caraway seeds, cooked outside on the grill, followed by the must of any gratar—miti, those little all-meat, fresh sausages cooked on the grill, and finally cozenat (a rolled up, sweet yeast bread), my American cookies (peanut butter) and more coffee and tuica and/or affinata (blueberry liqueur). Throughout the day, arriving guests would present their homemade alcoholic specialty (brandy, red and white wine, liqueur) and sampling was always a polite thing to do, of course.

Wednesday, June 1st, 2011

"Anca" and "Crina" are women of my village whom I know through observation, interactions, and snatches of conversation and to some extent through their children. They know little English and so we limp along with my little Romanian, and still I feel I know the quality of their character, and I admire them both. Anca is a woman in her late fifties, a kindergarten teacher and the mother of two lovely grown daughters. She is a bundle of energy and her bright henna-dyed hair and big smile make her easy to spot in a crowd. She not only deals with a passel of tiny tots all day, but she also tends a huge garden, and does massive canning and preserving of the produce as it's harvested. Her home is welcoming and well-organized. I love the fact that she has a fully-appointed wash stand between her garden and kitchen door and that she uses for handy hooks broken twig stumps on trees in her back yard. Her husband cannot eat dairy products and one of her daughters and son-in-law do not eat red meat. Still, from my experience, Anca's meals are delicious, varied and healthful (if one discounts the fried pies, which I do). At neighborhood celebrations she always has her kindergartners perform—recitations, dances, songs. I don't know how she trains them so well, but they're delightful to watch! At a performance of Romanian traditional music and dance in the city, Anca was the first on her feet, hand to her heart, when one of the singers began, "Rise, Romania, Rise," a rousing anthem. Having lived through the difficulties of her country's recent history, she holds dear her patriotism and pride. One of her daughters is in my adult class, speaks English, and is a very special young woman. Her intelligence and forward-looking attitude speak well for her up-bringing, and her affection and high regard for her mother are obvious . . . Crina is a neighbor, just a few doors down from the red house. I first met her when my landlady brought her up to meet me and make a request. We somehow communicated—neither of them speaking English and I with my baby-talk Romanian. She is a religion teacher (a mandatory subject here) at a school in the city, in her mid thirties, and her two children, Mihai (10) and Ioanna (7) attend schools in the city. She asked if I would spend some time talking with them. I explained that I cannot give private tutoring lessons (PC forbids it, rightfully), but that I would visit with them the next Saturday afternoon. What has evolved is a standing session at their house with her two children and often a few of their friends. I usually tailor for their level a lesson I presented that week to my classes. It became a highlight of my week, the children being precocious and delightful.

. . . Crina is one of the most poised people I've ever met. She is immensely attractive while being modest in her dress and demeanor. Her home is light and airy and aesthetically pleasing and her flower garden at the entrance to their home is nothing short of gorgeous. She speaks to me slowly and repeats as necessary, but (unlike me) she never uses her hands, keeping a very calm and serene tone. She has trained her children to be courteous and they always—on subtle command—present me with a little thank-you gift—as I'm leaving-usually chocolates or other sweets. Crina always follows me out to the gate and many times picks a bouquet on the way to send along with me. I have stayed for dinner on a few occasions and been royally treated with traditional foods. . . . She once said to me in the bleakness of January that I should come to see them any time and have a cup of tea, just visit, not be alone. I don't remember exactly how she said this to me, but I got it, and it endeared her to me, feeling that she saw me as a person a long way from home, and not just "the American woman."

Monday, June 6, 2011

The last of my mini portraits are of "Alina," one of my students, and "Bianca," a sales person at a local magazine. Alina is a pretty seventh grader who has the quiet grace and kindness of one much older. She seems "tuned in" to me and makes thoughtful gestures that sometimes catch me off guard. Mostly, she likes to accompany me on my walk home—or at least to HER home, which is about half way to mine. She will approach me after class and say "walk with you"? or at times on days I don't teach her, she'll simply be waiting a little way down the path. Sometimes her little brother, also a student, will be with her. I'm never sure if she's trying to help me with my Romanian or practice her English. We do both. I will ask *Cum se spune . . . ?* (how do you say?) about many items or phrases. She will ask me questions in English or just make an accurate statement at times that surprises me. She's one of those students you always feel deserves more. I admit there are days when I'm tired and feel I could use a quiet walk home, but I find that I always feel better after walking with Alina, waving her on at the corner where we part, feeling a little unspoken benediction in the "la revedere." I met Bianca the second day I was in the village, making my rounds to the magazins, introducing myself like a good little PCV. She seemed bemused and I immediately liked her bright, merry eyes and big smile. I know virtually nothing about this woman, but she has cheerfully helped me buy what I need two or three times a week. When I'm in the tiny store and others are there, she always introduces me if they seem curious—much smiling and nodding, and she gives me credit for learning Romanian *repede* (quickly—such a joke) when I ask properly for items, seeming to take a small measure of credit. We've had a few laughs, too. When I was doing some Christmas baking, I realized in the store that I was nearly out of baking powder and couldn't remember "praf de copt." Lee was with me and we both did numerous impressions of dough rising. Bianca thought we were hilarious (well, we were) and finally figured it out after pulling out nearly every little packet under the counter. She knows very well my taste in *vin alb* (white wine), the particular kind I like requiring her to fetch a little rickety ladder to reach it from the top shelf, and as she's reaching high (she's short) above her head, I and any number of other patrons are yelling for her to reach left or right to fetch it. I think what I really like about Bianca is her look of friendly expectancy, eyebrows raised and half-smile—as though my entering her little world could cause merriment at any moment. I live to serve.

Benediction of Romanian Women: A Sestina

She waits for me on the crumbled walk.
I see Alina's smile when her eyes find mine,
and more, a quiet knowing. How can a child
of fourteen years embody so much grace?
She will walk me home — a chance, no doubt,
to practice English, but it seems a benediction.

Raluca claps her hands with zeal, a comic benediction
that ends the appetizer course, and bids us take a country walk
while the men attend the grill. No one would doubt
her lively command, and the others' energies and mine
are stirred to leave the garden table, test our lady grace
in muddy shoes, and feel again the spring elation of a child.

Watching me as one would watch a child
with patient kindness fit for benediction,
Bianca also glows with expectation, for the grace
I wear into her store is often shed before I walk
away, reddened by friendly laughter, once more mining
from mental ore the fool's-gold words I should doubt.

Henna-bright and bustling, Anca leaves no doubt
she is the one in charge, yet even the most unruly child
could not deny that within her heart a mine
of gold yields undeserved and frequent benediction,
for in all she does as teacher, baker, gardener, she walks
each path in stone-solid faith her triumphs come by grace.

Within her well-kept home, Crina's presence summons grace.
Open-smiling, calm in manner, she erases all doubt
that I should march my foreign self up her front walk
each week to offer tutoring for her gentlemanly child.
Later, she escorts me through her garden, and as benediction
at the gate, she picks her finest blooms and makes them mine.

Flavia doesn't know her sterling worth. Constant friend of mine
who steadies as I stumble, she praises and then guides with grace
enough to camouflage the guiding. Double-kissing benediction,
she quietly manages, heals the hurt, removes the doubt.
With the intellect to master-teach and the heart to love each child,
she still declines to seek the prize and find the better walk.

If Fate were mine to bid and Justice balanced beyond doubt,
I'd give these six forever the grace of God, the wonder of a child,
and as benediction, a garden in Romania for their evening walk.

The River

For months I couldn't find it.
The description of the village
on a river prompted expectations:
the deep flow, the leafy banks,
afternoons of solitude.
When I asked, they'd point toward the north.

I walked north once in the fall —
a long walk from my house,
beyond the streets I knew, through high weeds
down a muddy path I thought was right.
I thought I smelled the water once.
At times the path disappeared where it looked
no different from the mumbling earth around it.
When it ended at the dump, I turned around
and looked for the way back,
broad plains and sky watching.

I asked my students in the spring
and they nodded yes,
they'd take me to the river.
"Will you?" I brightened.
But they never did.

That summer, a week before I left
the village, I found the river
as if by appointment,
dead reckoning my guide.
Approaching from my friends'
unfinished home on that village fringe
where I'd never been
and charged with the urgency of parting,
I angled north.

I could see it at last curving toward me
from the Carpathian source in the east and
away from me to the Hungarian plains in the west.
It rippled wide and shallow, gold-flecked
by the low sun. Yellow-green grasses swayed
above it on either side. Trees were scarce.
On a sand bar beneath a steep bank,
a family seemed to expand and contract.

I breathed in the open stretch of sky and plain
cut through by the reaching river,
and found I could carry away
enough, enough to say goodbye.

POSTLUDE

Monday, June 20th, 2011

Since I first began the long application process to be a volunteer in the Peace Corps in 2009, I've cringed whenever someone makes a comment about my "adventure." I know being a PC volunteer IS in the broad sense, an adventure ("an unusual experience," "a risky undertaking"), but in my mind there is a distinct difference between adventure and service. Adventure is something I do for myself. Service is something I do for others. And as corny as it sounds, service is the reason I joined the Peace Corps, leaving family and friends and a comfortable life to serve where I'm needed. So when news of a recent government study showing the low level of need for volunteers in Romania came to my attention last spring, I had to admit to myself that—in my particular village in my particular region, I had already reached that conclusion. This may not be true currently at all sites, but in a village where the school has perfectly competent English teachers and the mayor's pockets seem unusually deep, my presence is at best one of ambassadorship. At the same time, unplanned developments in my family and with some of my friends have created greater need for me back home. So when I put it all on the scale, the tilt was obvious and I just couldn't justify staying on in Romania to continue my "adventure." But oh, the difficulty of saying goodbye! I've repeatedly thought I'd like to be two people—one to go and one to stay. Because there are so many reasons I'd like to stay in this beautiful and complex country, enjoying its people, countryside, food, music, and traditions. I liked my Red House apartment, the big-sky sunsets, and many special people in my village and in the city. I became very close to my counterpart, a superb person professionally and personally. I'll miss my PCV colleagues, especially the Westsiders, and several others with whom I bonded during the training months. I sincerely hope my 60 blog entries have given my readers a good sense of what life in Romania is like and that I've represented my country well in my association with Romanians. I arrived back in America last Saturday night after teary goodbyes in Oradea to find teary hellos at the Atlanta airport. My heart is full and I know I'll be gleaning poems from this experience for a long while to come. Happily, I'll be returning to Romania in September with fellow Unitarian Universalists on a tour, so I was able to say "so long" instead of "goodbye" to several people I know I'll get to see then. And that trip will certainly be an adventure, something I'm doing for myself, a pleasure I look forward to.

Tuesday, October 4th, 2011

. . . The tour/pilgrimage ended with our leaving the village for Targu-Mures where the others would begin their return flights to the US. I, however, was given a ride to Cluj where I would take a train, probably my last in Romania, to Oradea to visit dear friends in the area.

My Last Train Ride in Romania

was supposed to be serene,
a nostalgic unwinding, winding
through countryside finally familiar
only to be left behind —
mountain passes,
pot-holed roads, sheep,
and the sweep of fields
strewn with plump new
haystacks, nestled villages,
steeples bright against trees,
and yellow daisies
nodding in the breeze of rails.
I plotted my sojourn,
three hours to meet this need
for farewell thoughts
and sighs, but not
for this surprise of Iulia.

She entered the car
mouth first, chattering loudly,
her mother in tow and useless
in the wake of her child of four.
For a full hour or more
I was Iulia's plaything, her seat
across from mine just fine
for sharing my almonds,
removing my sunglasses,
examining the tags
and zippers on my bag.

In baby Romanian
we offered names and ages.
Her eyes widened
at my accent, and

she got louder,
continually searching my eyes,
looking for
connection.
Irrepressible orb of confidence,
her round face bobbed
close to mine at times,
then down the aisle and back.
Her mother was absorbed
in passing hillsides.

But as they left, she told
her child to thank me,
which Iulia did, her hands
plastered with my monkey stickers,
her eyes already swinging to the exit
and beyond.
The remaining ride was quiet
and I did reflect,
but not on antiquated habits
of corruption and abuse,
those demons of this land.
I thought instead of hope.
I thought of Iulia's eyes.

Sunday, October 9th, 2011

The pull of friendship is strong and can shrink the globe in remarkable ways. Peace to all. May you be grateful citizens of this planet Earth. May you live a beautiful poem.

photo by Lee Reed

Clela Reed is the author of two books of poetry: *Dancing on the Rim* (Brick Road Poetry Press, 2009), *The Hero of the Revolution Serves Us Tea* (Negative Capability Press, 2014), and two chapbooks: *Bloodline* (Evening Street Press, 2009) and *Of Root and Sky* (Pudding House Publications, 2010). She has had poems published in *Caesura Literary Magazine, Colere Journal, The Kennesaw Review, Storysouth Journal, Clapboard House Literary Journal,* and others. A former English teacher and Facilitator for the Gifted, she recently returned from Peace Corps service in Romania during which she wrote weekly in a blog. She lives and writes with her husband and a small herd of deer in her forest home near Athens, Georgia.